THE RETIREMENT HANDBOOK FOR 60+

Your Complete Guide to Financial Security, Health, and Happiness in Your Golden Years

STEPHEN GORDON

ABOUT THE BOOK

"The Retirement Handbook for 60+" is a meticulously crafted guide designed to empower individuals approaching retirement age with the knowledge and tools necessary to navigate this significant life transition with confidence and clarity. This comprehensive handbook covers a wide range of topics essential for planning a secure and fulfilling retirement.

From financial planning strategies to legal considerations, healthcare options, and lifestyle adjustments, this book provides actionable advice tailored specifically for individuals aged 60 and above. Readers will learn how to optimize their retirement savings, maximize Social Security benefits, and create a sustainable budget that aligns with their lifestyle goals.

Beyond the realm of finances, this handbook delves into essential topics such as estate planning, long-term care options, and tax-efficient strategies to safeguard one's financial future. However, it doesn't stop there. It also offers guidance on nurturing physical and emotional well-being, engaging in meaningful activities, and cultivating fulfilling relationships in retirement.

What sets this book apart is its holistic approach to retirement planning, recognizing that true fulfillment in retirement extends beyond financial security. By providing expert advice, practical strategies, and inspirational insights, "The Retirement Handbook for 60+" empowers readers to embrace retirement as a time of growth, exploration, and fulfillment.

Whether you're just beginning to plan for retirement or are already in the midst of it, this handbook serves as an indispensable resource, offering clarity, confidence, and peace of mind as you embark on this exciting new chapter of life.

TABLE OF CONTENTS

INTRODUCTION

Welcome to "The Retirement Handbook for 60+." Retirement marks a significant milestone in our lives, a time of transition, reflection, and new beginnings. Whether you're eagerly anticipating the freedom that retirement brings or feeling apprehensive about the uncertainties ahead, this book is here to guide you through every step of the journey.

In the pages that follow, you'll find a wealth of invaluable information and expert advice tailored specifically for individuals aged 60 and above. The goal is simple: to empower you with the knowledge, tools, and confidence necessary to plan for a secure, fulfilling, and meaningful retirement.

Retirement planning encompasses a broad spectrum of considerations, from financial strategies and legal matters to lifestyle choices and healthcare decisions.

But this book is more than just a collection of facts and figures. It's a roadmap for embracing retirement as a time of opportunity, growth, and exploration. It's about envisioning the life you want to lead in retirement and taking proactive steps to make that vision a reality.

As you embark on this journey, I encourage you to approach retirement with an open mind and a spirit of adventure. Embrace the possibilities that lie ahead, and know that with the right knowledge and preparation, your retirement years can be the most fulfilling chapter of your life.

So let's begin. Turn the page and embark on this journey with me. Together, we'll chart a course for a retirement that's as vibrant and rewarding as you've always imagined.

CHAPTER ONE

Welcome to Retirement

Retirement marks a significant milestone in life, symbolizing the culmination of years of hard work and dedication. It's a time to bid farewell to the structured routine of the workplace and embrace a new chapter filled with possibilities, freedom, and exploration. As you embark on this journey, it's essential to approach retirement with a sense of excitement and anticipation, recognizing it as an opportunity to pursue your passions, deepen your relationships, and savor the moments that matter most.

Purpose and Scope of the Handbook

The purpose of "The Retirement Handbook for 60+" is to provide you with the essential knowledge, guidance, and resources you need to navigate the transition into retirement with confidence and clarity. This handbook is designed specifically for individuals aged 60 and above, recognizing the unique challenges and opportunities that come with this stage of life.

The scope is comprehensive, covering a wide range of topics relevant to retirement planning, including financial considerations, legal and estate planning, healthcare options, lifestyle choices, and emotional well-being. By addressing these key areas, the aim is to equip you with the tools and strategies necessary to make informed decisions and create a fulfilling retirement lifestyle tailored to your individual needs and preferences.

Navigating the contents of this handbook is simple, thanks to the carefully organized structure and user-friendly layout. Here's how you can make the most of your reading experience:

Read from Cover to Cover: Start by reading the book from beginning to end to gain a comprehensive understanding of the retirement planning process. Each chapter builds upon the previous one, guiding you through the various aspects of retirement planning in a logical and sequential manner.

Refer to Specific Chapters: If you have specific questions or concerns about certain aspects of retirement planning, feel free to skip to such chapters for targeted guidance and advice. The table of contents can help you quickly locate the information you need.

Take Notes and Reflect: As you read through the book, consider taking notes on key concepts, strategies, and action steps that resonate with you. Use these notes as a reference tool to guide your decision-making process and track your progress as you implement the recommendations outlined in the book.

Engage with the Material: Retirement planning is a dynamic and evolving process, and it's essential to engage actively with the material presented in this handbook. Take time to reflect on how the information applies to your unique situation, and be proactive in seeking additional resources and support as needed.

Share and Discuss: Retirement planning is not a solo endeavor, it's a journey that can benefit from the insights and perspectives of others. Consider sharing the insights gleaned from this handbook with your spouse, family members, or trusted advisors, and engage in meaningful discussions about your retirement goals and aspirations.

By following these guidelines, you'll be well-equipped to harness the power of "The Retirement Handbook for 60+" and embark on your retirement journey with confidence, clarity, and purpose. Congratulations on reaching this significant milestone, and best wishes for a fulfilling and rewarding retirement ahead!

Understanding Retirement in the 21st Century

Retirement in the 21st century is undergoing a profound transformation, shaped by shifting societal norms, economic dynamics, and demographic trends. As you navigate the complexities of retirement planning in this modern era, it's crucial to gain a comprehensive understanding of the factors influencing this evolution.

The Evolution of Retirement

The concept of retirement has evolved significantly over the years, transitioning from a relatively brief period of leisure at the end of one's working life to a more extended and multifaceted stage of life characterized by newfound freedoms and opportunities. Historically, retirement was often seen as a reward for a lifetime of labor, with individuals typically withdrawing from the workforce entirely upon reaching a certain age. However, in recent decades, retirement has become more fluid and flexible, with many people choosing to phase into retirement gradually or pursue second careers and entrepreneurial ventures in their later years.

Challenges and Opportunities

While retirement offers the promise of newfound freedom and leisure, it also presents a host of challenges and opportunities that must be navigated thoughtfully. Economic uncertainty, rising healthcare costs, and longevity risk are just a few of the financial challenges facing retirees today. Additionally, changes in family structures and social support systems can impact the retirement experience, as can advances in technology and shifts in the nature of work.

However, amidst these challenges lie opportunities for innovation, adaptation, and personal growth. With increased longevity and improved health outcomes, retirees have the opportunity to pursue lifelong passions, engage in meaningful volunteer work, and cultivate vibrant social networks. Furthermore, advancements in financial planning tools and retirement solutions empower individuals to take control of their financial futures and pursue their retirement goals with confidence.

Demographics and Trends

Demographic shifts, such as the aging of the baby boomer generation and declining birth rates in many developed countries, are reshaping the retirement landscape in profound ways. These demographic trends have far-reaching implications for retirement planning, from the sustainability of social security systems to the availability of healthcare services and the demand for retirement communities and long-term care facilities.

Moreover, cultural attitudes toward aging and retirement are evolving, with many individuals redefining what it means to grow older and embracing retirement as a time of reinvention and renewal. As the population continues to age and diversify, it's essential to recognize the diverse needs, preferences, and experiences of retirees from different backgrounds and walks of life.

In summary, understanding retirement in the 21st century requires a nuanced appreciation of the evolving dynamics shaping this stage of life. By recognizing the evolution of retirement, acknowledging the challenges and opportunities it presents, and staying attuned to demographic trends and cultural shifts, we can better prepare for the retirement journey and embrace this new chapter of life with confidence and optimism.

CHAPTER TWO

Financial Planning

Financial planning is a cornerstone of a successful retirement strategy, enabling individuals to assess their current financial situation, establish realistic goals, and develop a roadmap for achieving financial security in retirement. In this section, we'll explore key components of financial planning for retirement, including assessing your financial situation, budgeting, retirement income sources, investment strategies, and managing expenses.

Assessing Your Financial Situation

Before embarking on your retirement journey, it's essential to take stock of your current financial situation. This involves evaluating your assets, liabilities, income, and expenses to determine your net worth and assess your overall financial health. By understanding your financial standing, you can identify areas for improvement and develop a plan to achieve your retirement goals.

Budgeting for Retirement

Budgeting is a critical aspect of retirement planning, helping individuals manage their expenses and allocate resources effectively to meet their financial goals. In retirement, it's essential to create a realistic budget that accounts for essential expenses such as housing, healthcare, and utilities, as well as discretionary spending on leisure activities and travel. By establishing a budget and sticking to it, retirees can maintain financial stability and avoid running out of money in their later years.

Retirement Income Sources

Retirement income can come from various sources, including social security, pensions, and personal savings. Understanding and maximizing these income sources is key to ensuring a comfortable and secure retirement. In this section, we'll explore strategies for optimizing social security benefits, managing pension distributions, and leveraging retirement savings accounts such as 401(k)s and IRAs to generate income in retirement.

Social Security

Social Security is a foundational pillar of retirement income for many Americans, providing a reliable source of income throughout retirement. However, navigating the complexities of Social Security can be challenging, particularly when it comes to deciding when to claim benefits. In this section, we'll explore the factors to consider when claiming Social Security benefits and strategies for maximizing your benefits over the long term.

Pensions

Pensions are another common source of retirement income, particularly for individuals who have worked for employers offering pension plans. Understanding how pensions work, including distribution options and survivor benefits, is essential for maximizing this income stream in retirement. We'll discuss strategies for managing pension distributions and ensuring a steady stream of income throughout retirement.

Retirement Savings (401(k), IRA, etc.)

Personal savings, including retirement accounts such as 401(k)s and IRAs, play a crucial role in retirement planning. These accounts offer tax advantages and investment opportunities that can help individuals build a nest egg for retirement. In this section, we'll explore strategies for maximizing retirement savings contributions, choosing appropriate investment options, and managing withdrawals in retirement.

Investment Strategies for Seniors

Investment strategies for retirees differ from those employed during the accumulation phase of retirement planning. As individuals transition into retirement, their investment goals, risk tolerance, and time horizon may change. In this section, we'll explore investment strategies tailored to the needs of seniors, including asset allocation, risk management, and income generation strategies.

Managing Expenses in Retirement

Managing expenses is essential for maintaining financial stability in retirement. In this section, we'll discuss strategies for controlling costs, reducing debt, and adapting spending habits to align with retirement income sources. By prioritizing needs over wants and being mindful of discretionary spending, retirees can stretch their retirement savings further and enjoy a more secure financial future.

Planning for Healthcare Costs

Healthcare costs are a significant expense for many retirees, particularly as they age and require more extensive medical care. In this section, we'll explore strategies for managing healthcare costs in retirement, including purchasing supplemental insurance, setting aside funds for medical expenses, and exploring long-term care options. By planning for healthcare costs proactively, retirees can protect their financial security and enjoy peace of mind in retirement.

In conclusion, financial planning is a critical component of retirement preparation, enabling individuals to assess their financial situation, develop a realistic budget, and identify sources of retirement income. By understanding the various components of financial planning and implementing sound strategies for managing expenses and healthcare costs, retirees can achieve greater financial security and enjoy a more fulfilling retirement lifestyle.

CHAPTER THREE

Legal and Estate Planning

Legal and estate planning is essential for ensuring that your wishes are carried out and your assets are protected both during your lifetime and after your passing. In this section, we'll explore key components of legal and estate planning, including wills, trusts, powers of attorney, healthcare directives, long-term care planning, and understanding government healthcare programs such as Medicare and Medicaid.

Wills, Trusts, and Estate Planning Basics

A will is a legal document that outlines how you want your assets to be distributed upon your death and appoints a personal representative to oversee the distribution process. Trusts, on the other hand, are legal arrangements that allow you to transfer assets to beneficiaries while bypassing probate and providing greater control over how those assets are managed. In this section, we'll discuss the basics of wills, trusts, and estate planning and explore strategies for protecting your assets and minimizing estate taxes.

Power of Attorney and Healthcare Directives

A power of attorney is a legal document that grants someone the authority to make financial decisions on your behalf if you become incapacitated. Healthcare directives, also known as living wills or advance directives, outline your preferences for medical treatment in the event that you are unable to communicate your wishes. In this section, we'll discuss the importance of establishing powers of attorney and healthcare directives and provide guidance on how to create these documents effectively.

Long-Term Care Planning

Long-term care planning involves preparing for the possibility of needing assistance with activities of daily living as you age. Long-term care services can be expensive, and without proper planning, the costs can quickly deplete your savings. In this section, we'll explore long-term care insurance options, Medicaid planning strategies, and other resources available to help cover the costs of long-term care.

Understanding Medicare and Medicaid

Medicare and Medicaid are government healthcare programs designed to provide coverage for eligible individuals, particularly seniors and those with low incomes.

Understanding how these programs work and what benefits they provide is essential for ensuring that you have access to the healthcare services you need in retirement. In this section, we'll discuss the differences between Medicare and Medicaid, eligibility requirements, coverage options, and enrollment considerations.

In conclusion, legal and estate planning is a critical component of retirement preparation, enabling individuals to protect their assets, ensure their wishes are carried out, and plan for their long-term care needs. By understanding the basics of wills, trusts, powers of attorney, healthcare directives, and government healthcare programs such as Medicare and Medicaid, retirees can achieve greater peace of mind and enjoy a more secure financial future.

Lifestyle Considerations

Retirement is not just about financial planning; it's also an opportunity to design a lifestyle that reflects your values, interests, and aspirations. In this section, we'll explore various lifestyle considerations that can enhance your retirement experience and contribute to your overall well-being and fulfillment.

Health and Wellness in Retirement

Maintaining good health and wellness is essential for enjoying a vibrant and active retirement lifestyle. In this section, we'll discuss strategies for staying physically active, eating a balanced diet, managing stress, and prioritizing preventive healthcare measures. By making health and wellness a priority, retirees can enjoy a higher quality of life and remain independent and active for years to come.

Social and Community Engagement

Social connections are vital for emotional well-being and fulfillment in retirement. Engaging with friends, family, and community organizations can provide a sense of belonging, purpose, and support. In this section, we'll explore ways to build and maintain social connections in retirement, including joining clubs and organizations, volunteering, and participating in social activities and events.

Hobbies, Travel, and Leisure Activities

Retirement offers the freedom to pursue hobbies, interests, and leisure activities that may have been neglected during your working years. Whether it's gardening, painting, golfing, or traveling, retirement provides ample opportunities to explore new passions and enjoy life to the fullest. In this section, we'll discuss strategies for discovering new hobbies, planning travel adventures, and incorporating leisure activities into your retirement routine.

Downsizing and Housing Options

As retirees age, they may find that their housing needs change. Downsizing to a smaller home or relocating to a retirement community can offer financial benefits, reduce maintenance responsibilities, and provide access to amenities and services designed specifically for seniors. In this section, we'll explore downsizing and housing options for retirees, including independent living communities, assisted living facilities, and continuing care retirement communities.

Giving back to the community through volunteer work and philanthropy can provide a sense of purpose, fulfillment, and social connection in retirement. Whether it's mentoring young people, serving meals at a local shelter, or supporting charitable organizations, retirees have a wealth of opportunities to make a positive impact on the world around them. In this section, we'll discuss ways to get involved in volunteer and philanthropic activities and the benefits of giving back to others.

In conclusion, lifestyle considerations play a significant role in shaping the retirement experience and contributing to overall well-being and fulfillment. By prioritizing health and wellness, nurturing social connections, pursuing hobbies and leisure activities, exploring housing options, and engaging in volunteer and philanthropic endeavors, retirees can create a lifestyle that reflects their values, interests, and aspirations, and enjoy a fulfilling and meaningful retirement journey.

CHAPTER FOUR

Psychological and Emotional Well-being

Psychological and emotional well-being are integral aspects of a fulfilling and satisfying retirement. As individuals transition from the workforce to retirement, they may encounter a range of emotional challenges and opportunities. In this section, we'll explore strategies for adjusting to retirement, coping with transitions and loss, maintaining mental acuity and cognitive health, and building meaningful relationships in later life.

Adjusting to Retirement

Retirement represents a significant life transition that can evoke a mix of emotions, including excitement, apprehension, and uncertainty. Adjusting to retirement involves adapting to changes in routine, identity, and social connections. In this section, we'll discuss strategies for navigating the emotional ups and downs of retirement, finding a sense of purpose and meaning, and embracing the opportunities for growth and exploration that retirement affords.

Coping with Transitions and Loss

Retirement often coincides with other life transitions, such as changes in health, family dynamics, or personal relationships. Additionally, retirees may experience losses, such as the death of a spouse or loved one, that can profoundly impact their emotional well-being. In this section, we'll explore strategies for coping with transitions and loss, including seeking support from friends and family, practicing self-care, and finding meaning and resilience in the face of adversity.

Maintaining Mental Acuity and Cognitive Health

As individuals age, maintaining mental acuity and cognitive health becomes increasingly important for preserving independence and quality of life. In this section, we'll discuss strategies for keeping the mind sharp and engaged, including engaging in intellectually stimulating activities, staying physically active, and adopting healthy lifestyle habits. We'll also explore the role of lifelong learning and brain training exercises in promoting cognitive vitality in later life.

Building Meaningful Relationships in Later Life

Social connections play a vital role in psychological and emotional well-being, particularly in later life. Building and nurturing meaningful relationships can provide a sense of belonging, support, and companionship in retirement. In this section, we'll discuss strategies for cultivating new friendships, strengthening existing relationships, and finding community and connection through social activities, clubs, and organizations.

In conclusion, psychological and emotional well-being are essential components of a fulfilling and satisfying retirement. By embracing strategies for adjusting to retirement, coping with transitions and loss, maintaining mental acuity and cognitive health, and building meaningful relationships in later life, retirees can enhance their overall quality of life and enjoy a more fulfilling retirement journey.

Navigating Social Security and Medicare

Navigating Social Security and Medicare is a crucial aspect of retirement planning, as these government programs provide essential benefits and coverage for retirees. In this section, we'll explore strategies for maximizing Social Security benefits, understanding Medicare coverage and enrollment, and exploring supplemental insurance options to enhance your healthcare coverage in retirement.

Maximizing Social Security Benefits

Social Security benefits provide a foundation of income for many retirees, but the timing of when to claim benefits can significantly impact the amount you receive. In this section, we'll discuss strategies for maximizing Social Security benefits, including understanding the factors that affect benefit amounts, deciding when to claim benefits based on your individual circumstances, and optimizing spousal and survivor benefits.

Understanding Medicare Coverage and Enrollment

Medicare is a federal health insurance program that provides coverage for eligible individuals aged 65 and older, as well as some younger individuals with disabilities or specific medical conditions. Understanding Medicare coverage options, enrollment deadlines, and eligibility requirements is essential for ensuring access to healthcare services in retirement. In this section, we'll provide an overview of Medicare Parts A, B, C, and D, discuss enrollment periods and eligibility criteria, and explore coverage options for prescription drugs and preventive services.

Supplemental Insurance Options

While Medicare provides comprehensive coverage for many healthcare services, it doesn't cover all expenses, and out-of-pocket costs can add up quickly. Supplemental insurance, such as Medicare Supplement (Medigap) plans and Medicare Advantage plans, can help fill in the gaps in Medicare coverage and provide additional benefits and protections. In this section, we'll discuss the differences between Medigap and Medicare Advantage plans, explore the benefits and drawbacks of each option, and provide guidance on choosing the right supplemental insurance coverage for your needs.

In conclusion, navigating Social Security and Medicare is a critical aspect of retirement planning, and understanding your options can help you make informed decisions about your healthcare coverage in retirement. By maximizing Social Security benefits, understanding Medicare coverage and enrollment, and exploring supplemental insurance options, you can ensure access to quality healthcare services and protect your financial security in retirement.

CHAPTER FIVE

Tax Strategies for Seniors

Tax planning is an essential aspect of retirement planning, as it can significantly impact your financial security and the overall success of your retirement. In this section, we'll explore tax considerations in retirement, deductions and credits available to seniors, and tax-efficient withdrawal strategies to help you minimize your tax liability and maximize your retirement savings.

Tax Considerations in Retirement

Retirement brings about changes in your income sources and financial situation, which can have implications for your tax obligations. Understanding the tax implications of different retirement income sources, such as Social Security benefits, pensions, retirement account withdrawals, and investment income, is crucial for effective tax planning. In this section, we'll discuss how different types of retirement income are taxed and explore strategies for minimizing your tax liability in retirement.

Deductions and Credits for Seniors

Seniors may be eligible for various tax deductions and credits that can help reduce their tax burden and maximize their retirement savings. Common deductions and credits for seniors include the standard deduction for taxpayers over 65, the additional standard deduction for blind individuals, the Elderly and Disabled Tax Credit, and deductions for medical expenses and property taxes. In this section, we'll explore these deductions and credits in detail and provide guidance on how to take advantage of them to lower your tax bill.

Withdrawals from retirement accounts, such as traditional IRAs and 401(k) plans, are typically subject to income tax. However, by employing tax-efficient withdrawal strategies, you can minimize the tax impact of your withdrawals and optimize your retirement income. Strategies such as Roth IRA conversions, tax bracket management, and strategic asset allocation can help you manage your tax liability while maximizing the longevity of your retirement savings. In this section, we'll discuss these strategies and provide guidance on how to implement them effectively to achieve your retirement goals.

In conclusion, tax planning is a critical component of retirement planning, and seniors can benefit from understanding the tax considerations specific to their retirement years.

By taking advantage of deductions and credits for seniors, exploring tax-efficient withdrawal strategies, and staying informed about changes in tax laws and regulations, retirees can minimize their tax liability and make the most of their retirement savings.

Planning for Long-Term Care

Long-term care planning is a crucial aspect of retirement planning, as it involves preparing for the possibility of needing assistance with activities of daily living as you age. In this section, we'll explore strategies for assessing long-term care needs, options for financing long-term care, including long-term care insurance, and alternative care options for retirees.

Assessing Long-Term Care Needs

Assessing long-term care needs involves evaluating your current health status, family history, lifestyle factors, and preferences to determine the level of care you may require in the future. Factors to consider include mobility, cognitive function, chronic health conditions, and support networks. By understanding your long-term care needs, you can develop a plan to address potential challenges and ensure access to appropriate care and support services as you age.

Long-Term Care Insurance

Long-term care insurance is a type of insurance policy designed to cover the costs of long-term care services, such as nursing home care, assisted living, and in-home care. Long-term care insurance can provide financial protection and peace of mind by helping to cover the high costs of long-term care services, which can quickly deplete retirement savings. In this section, we'll explore how long-term care insurance works, factors to consider when purchasing a policy, and alternatives to traditional long-term care insurance.

Alternative Care Options

In addition to long-term care insurance, retirees have a range of alternative care options to consider, depending on their needs and preferences. These options may include home health care services, adult day care programs, assisted living facilities, and continuing care retirement communities. Alternative care options offer flexibility, allowing individuals to receive care in a setting that best meets their needs while maintaining independence and quality of life. In this section, we'll discuss different types of alternative care options, their benefits and drawbacks, and factors to consider when evaluating these options.

In conclusion, planning for long-term care is an essential component of retirement planning, as it involves preparing for the possibility of needing assistance with activities of daily living as you age. By assessing long-term care needs, exploring long-term care insurance options, and considering alternative care options, retirees can develop a comprehensive plan to address their long-term care needs and protect their financial security in retirement.

CHAPTER SIX

Legacy and End-of-Life Planning

Legacy and end-of-life planning involves preparing for the future and ensuring that your wishes are carried out with regard to your personal legacy, funeral arrangements, and communicating important information to loved ones. In this section, we'll explore strategies for leaving a lasting legacy, planning for funeral and burial arrangements, and effectively communicating your wishes to loved ones.

Leaving a Lasting Legacy

Leaving a legacy involves more than just passing on material possessions; it's about sharing your values, beliefs, and life lessons with future generations. Whether it's through charitable donations, philanthropic endeavors, or creating a family history or memoir, there are many ways to leave a meaningful and lasting legacy. In this section, we'll explore strategies for identifying your values and priorities, determining how you want to be remembered, and taking proactive steps to leave a positive impact on future generations.

Funeral and Burial Planning

Funeral and burial planning involves making decisions about how you want your final arrangements to be handled and ensuring that your wishes are carried out with dignity and respect. By planning ahead, you can alleviate the burden on your loved ones and ensure that your final wishes are honored. In this section, we'll discuss considerations for funeral and burial planning, including choosing a funeral home, selecting burial or cremation options, and pre arranging funeral services.

Effective communication is essential for ensuring that your wishes are understood and respected by your loved ones. By openly discussing your end-of-life preferences and sharing important information about your wishes, you can provide clarity and peace of mind for yourself and your family members. In this section, we'll explore strategies for initiating conversations about end-of-life planning, communicating your wishes effectively, and documenting important information for your loved ones to reference in the future.

In conclusion, legacy and end-of-life planning are important aspects of comprehensive retirement planning, as they involve preparing for the future and ensuring that your wishes are carried out with regard to your personal legacy, funeral arrangements, and communication with loved ones. By taking proactive steps to leave a lasting legacy, plan for funeral and burial arrangements, and communicate your wishes effectively, you can achieve peace of mind and ensure that your wishes are honored in the future.

Financial Planning Calculators and Tools

Retirement Savings Calculator: Helps estimate how much you need to save for retirement based on factors such as age, income, and retirement goals.

Social Security Benefit Estimator: Allows you to calculate your estimated Social Security benefits based on your earnings history and projected retirement age.

401(k) and IRA Contribution Calculators: Helps determine how much you should contribute to your retirement accounts to reach your savings goals.

Budgeting and Expense Tracking Tools: Tools like Mint or Personal Capital can help you track your expenses, set budget goals, and manage your finances more effectively.

Support Groups and Community Services

1. AARP Community: AARP offers online forums and local chapters where retirees can connect with peers, share experiences, and access resources and support.

2. Local Senior Centers: Many communities have senior centers that offer a variety of programs, activities, and services for older

adults, including social events, educational workshops, and wellness programs.

3. Alzheimer's Association Support Groups: For individuals dealing with dementia or caring for loved ones with dementia, the Alzheimer's Association offers support groups, educational resources, and caregiver training programs.

4. Eldercare Locator: A service provided by the U.S. Administration on Aging that helps older adults and their families find local resources and support services, such as transportation assistance, meal programs, and legal aid services.

In conclusion, connecting with support groups and community services can greatly enhance your retirement planning experience and provide valuable support as you navigate this important life transition. By leveraging these you can make informed decisions, set realistic goals, and enjoy a fulfilling and rewarding retirement journey.

Reflecting on Your Retirement Journey

As you embark on your retirement journey, take a moment to reflect on the path that has led you to this significant milestone. Consider the successes you've achieved, the challenges you've overcome, and the lessons you've learned along the way. Reflecting on your retirement journey can provide valuable insights and perspective as you transition into this new phase of life.

Think about the goals and aspirations you have for your retirement years. What are the activities, experiences, and accomplishments that will bring you joy and fulfillment? Take the time to envision the life you want to lead in retirement and set clear intentions for how you will pursue your dreams and aspirations.

Remember that retirement is not just about financial planning; it's also about emotional well-being, personal growth, and meaningful connections. Cultivate a sense of gratitude for the opportunities and blessings in your life, and embrace the challenges as opportunities for growth and transformation.

Final Words of Advice

As you embark on your retirement journey, I offer the following words of advice:

1. Prioritize Your Health and Well-being: Your health is your most valuable asset in retirement. Prioritize self-care, stay active, eat well, and seek regular medical check-ups to maintain your physical and emotional well-being.

2. Stay Engaged and Active: Retirement is a time to explore new interests, pursue passions, and stay engaged in meaningful activities. Stay connected with friends, family, and community, and seek out opportunities for personal growth and enrichment.

3. Be Flexible and Open-minded: Retirement is a journey filled with unexpected twists and turns. Embrace flexibility and open-mindedness as you navigate the changes and challenges that come your way, and remain adaptable to new opportunities and experiences.

4. Plan for the Unexpected: Life is unpredictable, and it's essential to have contingency plans in place for unexpected events or emergencies. Build a robust financial plan, establish a support network, and stay informed about resources and services available to you.

5. Celebrate Your Achievements: Take time to celebrate your achievements and milestones along the way. Reflect on your accomplishments, express gratitude for the experiences you've had, and savor the moments of joy and fulfillment that retirement brings.

In closing, remember that retirement is a journey, not a destination. Embrace the opportunities for growth, discovery, and connection that retirement offers, and cherish the moments spent with loved ones and pursuing your passions. May your retirement be filled with happiness, fulfillment, and abundance in all aspects of life.

CHAPTER SEVEN

Appendix

Glossary of Retirement Terms

Retirement planning involves navigating a complex landscape of financial concepts and terminology. To aid in your understanding of key terms and concepts related to retirement, this glossary provides definitions and explanations of commonly used terms in retirement planning and financial management.

1. 401(k) Plan: A retirement savings plan sponsored by an employer that allows employees to contribute a portion of their salary to a tax-advantaged investment account for retirement savings.

2. Annuity: A financial product typically offered by insurance companies that provides a stream of income payments over a specified period, often used as part of retirement income planning.

3. Asset Allocation: The distribution of investment assets across different asset classes, such as stocks, bonds, and cash, to achieve a desired level of risk and return in a portfolio.

4. Defined Benefit Plan: A retirement plan sponsored by an employer that provides employees with a predetermined retirement benefit based on factors such as salary and years of service.

5. Defined Contribution Plan: A retirement plan sponsored by an employer that allows employees to make contributions to individual

accounts, typically with employer matching contributions, such as 401(k) plans.

6. IRA (Individual Retirement Account): A tax-advantaged investment account designed to help individuals save for retirement, with options including traditional IRAs, Roth IRAs, and SEP IRAs.

7. Medicare: A federal health insurance program for individuals aged 65 and older (and certain younger individuals with disabilities), providing coverage for hospitalization, medical services, and prescription drugs.

8. Required Minimum Distribution (RMD): The minimum amount that retirees must withdraw from their retirement accounts, such as traditional IRAs and 401(k) plans, each year once they reach a certain age (currently 72 for most retirees).

9. Roth Conversion: The process of transferring funds from a traditional IRA or employer-sponsored retirement plan to a Roth IRA, typically subject to income taxes in the year of conversion.

10. Social Security: A federal program that provides retirement, disability, and survivor benefits to eligible individuals based on their work history and contributions to the Social Security system.

11. Target-Date Fund: A mutual fund or investment option designed to automatically adjust its asset allocation over time to become more conservative as the target retirement date approaches.

12. Withdrawal Strategy: A plan for systematically withdrawing funds from retirement accounts to meet income needs in

retirement while minimizing taxes and preserving the longevity of retirement savings.

This glossary is intended to serve as a reference guide to help you navigate the terminology and concepts associated with retirement planning. As you continue your journey toward retirement, refer to this appendix to deepen your understanding and make informed decisions about your financial future.

Sample Documents and Forms

As part of your retirement planning journey, you may encounter various documents and forms that are integral to managing your finances and preparing for retirement. This section provides a collection of sample documents and forms commonly used in retirement planning and financial management.

1. Retirement Account Statements: Sample statements from retirement accounts, such as 401(k) plans, IRAs, and pension accounts, showing account balances, contributions, and investment performance.

2. Social Security Statement: A sample Social Security statement from the Social Security Administration (SSA), providing an estimate of future Social Security benefits based on your earnings history and projected retirement age.

3. Budget Worksheet: A sample budget worksheet to help you assess your current expenses, identify areas for savings, and develop a budget for retirement income and expenses.

4. Retirement Income Projection: A sample retirement income projection spreadsheet, showing estimated income from various

sources, including Social Security, pensions, and retirement savings accounts.

5. Beneficiary Designation Form: A sample beneficiary designation form for retirement accounts, allowing you to designate beneficiaries to receive the assets in your retirement accounts upon your death.

6. Power of Attorney Form: A sample power of attorney form, allowing you to appoint someone to make financial decisions on your behalf if you become incapacitated.

7. Healthcare Directive/Living Will: A sample healthcare directive or living will form, allowing you to specify your wishes for medical treatment and end-of-life care in the event that you are unable to communicate your preferences.

8. Long-Term Care Insurance Policy: A sample long-term care insurance policy document, outlining the terms and conditions of coverage for long-term care services.

9. Medicare Enrollment Form: A sample Medicare enrollment form for individuals aged 65 and older, allowing you to enroll in Medicare Parts A and B and select additional coverage options, such as Medicare Advantage or prescription drug plans.

10. Estate Planning Documents: Sample estate planning documents, including wills, trusts, and advance directives, to help you create a comprehensive estate plan and ensure that your wishes are carried out upon your death.

These sample documents and forms are provided for informational purposes only and should be used as reference materials in conjunction with professional advice from qualified financial and legal professionals. As you navigate your retirement planning journey, consult with professionals to ensure that your documents and forms are tailored to your specific needs and circumstances.

CONCLUSION

As we reach the conclusion of "The Retirement Handbook for 60+," I hope that you've found the guidance and resources within these pages invaluable as you plan for your retirement journey. Retirement is not just a destination, it's a new chapter filled with opportunities for growth, exploration, and fulfillment.

Throughout this handbook, together we've explored the myriad considerations that come with retirement planning, from financial strategies and legal matters to lifestyle choices and healthcare decisions. I've provided practical advice, expert insights, and actionable steps to help you navigate this complex terrain with confidence and clarity.

But beyond the practical aspects of retirement planning, I've also emphasized the importance of embracing retirement as a time of personal growth and fulfillment. Retirement offers the chance to pursue passions, cultivate meaningful relationships, and explore new interests. It's an opportunity to redefine what success means to you and to create a life that aligns with your values and aspirations.

As you move forward on your retirement journey, we encourage you to approach this new chapter of your life with optimism, curiosity, and a spirit of adventure. Remember that retirement is not the end of the road, it's the beginning of a new and exciting chapter.

I extend my heartfelt wishes for a retirement filled with joy, fulfillment, and abundance. May you seize each day with enthusiasm and embrace the possibilities that lie ahead. And remember, the journey doesn't end here. As you navigate the ups and downs of retirement, know that you have the knowledge, resources, and support you need to thrive.

Thank you for entrusting me with your retirement planning journey. I wish you all the best as you embark on this next chapter of your life.

Warm regards,

APPRECIATION

As the author of "The Retirement Handbook for 60+," it is my privilege and honor to share this journey with you. Retirement planning is a deeply personal and often complex endeavor, and I've poured my insights, and experiences into crafting this handbook to serve as your trusted companion along the way.

My motivation for writing this book stems from a genuine desire to empower individuals aged 60 and above with the knowledge and resources they need to navigate the transition into retirement with confidence and clarity.

I understand the myriad challenges and uncertainties that can arise during this phase of life, and my goal is to provide you with practical guidance and actionable advice to help you navigate those challenges with ease.

I recognize that every individual's journey into retirement is unique, shaped by personal goals, values, and circumstances. That's why I've taken a holistic approach to retirement planning, addressing not only the financial aspects but also the emotional, social, and lifestyle considerations that are integral to a fulfilling retirement.

Throughout this book, I've drawn upon my expertise in financial planning, legal matters, healthcare, and psychology, as well as insights gleaned from years of working closely with individuals transitioning into retirement.

My hope is that the information presented here will not only inform your decisions but also inspire you to embrace retirement as a time of opportunity, growth, and exploration.

I understand that retirement planning can be overwhelming at times, but I want to reassure you that you are not alone on this journey. I'm here to support you every step of the way, and I invite you to reach out with any questions, concerns, or insights you may have as you work through the material in this handbook.

In closing, I want to express once again my heartfelt gratitude to you, the reader, for entrusting me with your retirement planning journey. It is my sincere hope that this book will serve as a valuable resource and companion as you embark on this exciting new chapter of your life.

Warm regards,

STEPHEN GORDON